ACTIVISTS ASSEMBLE

SAVE *YOUR* PLANET

BEN HOARE   JADE ORLANDO

For my
two little Earth Heroes,
and all the other children who
believe in a cleaner, fairer,
greener future - B.H.

For every child who
wants a beautiful, healthy home
on our planet earth - J.O.

First published 2021 by Macmillan Children's Books
an imprint of Pan Macmillan
The Smithson, 6 Briset Street, London, EC1M 5NR
Associated companies throughout the world
www.panmacmillan.com

ISBN 978-0-7534-4620-1

Text copyright © Macmillan Publishers International Ltd 2021
Illustration copyright © Jade Orlando 2021

Designed by Ailsa Cullen
Edited by Catherine Brereton

Ben Hoare and Jade Orlando have asserted their rights to be
identified as the author and illustrator of this work in
accordance with the Copyright, Designs and Patents Act 1988.

2 4 6 8 9 7 5 3 1

A CIP catalogue record for this book
is available from the British Library.

Printed in China

CONTENTS

Introduction 4

Population 6

HABITAT AND HUNTING

Habitat Loss 8

Hunting 10

Wildlife Trade 12

CLIMATE CHANGE

Changing World 14

Tackling Climate Change 16

Climate Change Solutions 18

FOOD

Food and Farming 20

Fishing 22

Meat Eating 24

POLLUTION

Air Pollution 26

Pollution of Land and Sea 28

Plastic Peril 30

AT HOME

Energy in the Home 32

Water for All 34

Earth Activism in your own Back Yard 36

CITIES AND TRAVEL

Shopping 38

Green Cities 40

Flying 42

Hope: A Greener Future 44

Glossary 46

Index 48

ACTIVITIES

Discussion Time 49

Quiz 54

Find Out 56

Get Active 58

Writing and Drawing Activities 60

THERE IS NO PLANET "B"

INTRODUCTION

Earth is beautiful. As far as we know, it is also the only planet that can support life. It's our home, and we need to look after it.

There are millions of species on Earth, from the mighty blue whale to tiny bacteria too small to see. There could be around nine million species, maybe more. Most are still out there, waiting to be discovered. But one species towers over all others. Us.

Human beings are a great success story. We can survive almost everywhere. This is because we know how to make tools, houses, clothes and vehicles, and because we know how to grow food and generate power. Some scientists call the time we now live in the "Age of Humans".

So it is easy to forget that we are part of nature and depend on it. We rely on nature for every breath we take, every drop we drink and every mouthful we eat. Everything we make – even tarmac and concrete, steel and plastic – comes from the natural world, too.

Like a human body, Earth is only healthy if all its parts are working properly. But we have destroyed many of its natural habitats. We have lost half the world's wildlife over the past 50 years. We dump our waste on the land and at sea. We pour smoke and chemicals into the air. We are also, by our actions, changing the world's climate.

This book looks at the main challenges facing the environment. How can we protect precious habitats and save wildlife? How can we produce food and make things without harming the natural world? How can we cut down on waste and pollution?

This book will also help you to think about some of the answers. We need to work with nature, not against it. We need to learn to live more gently on the planet. Change starts with you. Your family. Your friends. Together, we can save the planet!

"We already have all the facts and solutions. All we have to do is wake up and change." Greta Thunberg

POPULATION

The number of people on Earth has shot up. This is having a massive impact on the planet and its wildlife. To save the planet, the enormous human population is one of the biggest problems we have to overcome.

Wealthy countries take most from the natural world. If everyone on Earth lived like the population of the USA, for example, we would need four extra Earths to keep up with our demands.

In 1950, the world's population was 2.6 billion. In 2020, it was 7.8 billion. The growth rate is now slowing down. Even so, experts think that by 2050 there could be 9.7 billion people. That's like adding 200,000 extra people every single day until the middle of this century.

Everyone needs a home, food and fresh water, and we use energy for cooking, heating, lighting, transport and much else besides. In the end, all these things come from nature. But supplies are limited, because we only have one Earth. So as the human population grows, it puts more pressure on the natural world.

SiR DAViD ATTENBOROUGH
(BORN 1926)

More than anyone else, this English TV presenter has spread the word about why we need nature and why we must protect it. His wildlife programmes have been enjoyed by many millions of people around the globe. They include hits such as *Life on Earth*, *Planet Earth* and *Planet Earth II*, and *The Blue Planet* and *Blue Planet II*. Sir David often speaks up about the threats to the world, and why its growing human population is a huge issue. He has said that all of our problems are easier to solve with fewer people on the planet, and harder with more people.

ECOLOGICAL FOOTPRINT

The amount we take from nature is called our ecological footprint. This is a measure of how much land and water is needed to keep us alive and deal with our waste. The more land and water we use, the larger the ecological footprint.

Can we find ways to shrink our ecological footprint? Then the natural world will be under less pressure. The planet will be healthier, with more space for wildlife. One way to do this is to change how we live. For example, we could buy fewer products and make them last longer. We could create less waste. We could redesign our homes and cities. We could travel less, and we could consider changing our diet.

HABITAT LOSS

Earth is made up of many special worlds called habitats. These range from a mighty mountain or grassland to a hedge or puddle. Each habitat is home to different plants, animals and other living things. If we damage or destroy it, these species are left homeless. As more habitat is lost, they become rare, or endangered. Eventually some die out, or go extinct.

People need land for houses, cities and factories, and to grow crops. So we clear forests, drain marshes and plough up grasslands. We also dig mines to excavate rock and minerals. We build roads and railways that carve the land up even further. Habitat destruction happens at sea, too. For example, fishing nets and oil pipelines can harm the fragile seabed.

There are excellent ways of saving habitats. One is to set up nature reserves, national parks and marine protected areas. Here, there is more space for wildlife and strict limits on what people can do. Governments can also pass laws that protect species and their habitats.

AMAZING RAINFOREST

The Amazon in South America is the world's largest rainforest. Nowhere else has this many species, from jaguars and howler monkeys to colourful parrots. The forest's 400 billion trees pump so much oxygen and water into the air that they help to control Earth's climate. People call the Amazon the "lungs of the planet".

But this wonderful rainforest is fast being cleared. People want to take its valuable wood, and to use the land for beef cattle and crops such as soya, and for gold mining. One fifth of the forest has been lost in 50 years.

MARINA SILVA
(BORN 1958)

As a girl growing up in a poor family in Brazil, Marina saw with her own eyes the damage being done to the Amazon. She realized that clearing the land mainly helped a few rich people, who became even richer. So she organized peaceful protests. Later, she became a popular politician. From 2003 to 2008, she was a Brazilian government minister and helped to pass stronger laws to protect the rainforest. Now the destruction has got worse again, but still this hero fights on.

HUNTING

In the beginning, until about 12,000 years ago, early humans were hunter-gatherers. They hunted animals and gathered seeds, fruit and other plant foods. They used spears, bows and arrows and axes, taking just what they needed.

Take-what-you-need hunting still exists in a few parts of the world. But today, the human population is much larger, and most hunting is not like this. Too many wild animals are killed, and their populations start to get smaller.

THE HUNTED

Around the globe, people hunt all kinds of wildlife, from deer and ducks to monkeys and seals. Fishing is a type of hunting, too. Often wild animals are caught for their meat, fur or ivory, but some are taken as sport. Many animals are shot or poisoned because they are seen as pests. Others, such as bats and snakes, are killed just because people are afraid of them.

Thousands of species are at risk of disappearing forever. So many are going extinct that scientists call it an extinction crisis. Hunting is a major cause of this emergency.

Many people are against hunting. One common argument is that it is cruel. People say, "We have no right to kill another creature!" In some cases it may be possible to hunt wild animals without putting their whole population in danger. But only if people are careful and follow the rules.

To protect wildlife, we can limit how many animals are taken each year or each season. This is called sustainable hunting. In some areas, such as nature reserves, no hunting or fishing is ever allowed. For rare species, we might need to stop it everywhere. Nature soon recovers if we leave it in peace. Unfortunately, some people break the law. Illegal hunting of wildlife is a huge problem.

GIANT NEWS

Fishing fleets used to catch enormous numbers of whales. Then, in 1986, after a massive global "Save the Whales" campaign, hunting whales was banned all over the world. Now numbers of humpback whales and other big whales are going up again. There are more whales swimming in the big blue than for 100 years! But Japan, Norway and Iceland don't agree with the ban, and still hunt whales.

WILDLIFE TRADE

All through history,
we have taken plants and
animals from the wild to sell them.
Today, this trade is worth billions of dollars.
People buy and sell everything from bones, fur
and shells to flowers and snakeskin. Live animals are
caught for circuses and aquariums and for sale as pets.

Some wildlife trade is legal, but much of it is not. It's big
business, often run by gangs of criminals. To crack down on
the illegal trade, many countries employ guards in national
parks and do checks at airports. Those who break the
law risk heavy fines and may even go to prison.

Elephants and rhinos are killed
for their ivory. This is turned into
powder, which is sold in China and
other parts of Asia as an expensive
"medicine". It doesn't work, because
ivory is made of the same stuff as
human hair and fingernails. But
still the ivory trade continues. As a
result, all of the world's elephants
and rhinos are under threat.

TACKLING THE PROBLEM

The illegal wildlife trade is a problem that affects all countries, so we need to find ways to control it. Conservationists put a lot of effort into education. If more people understand how serious the problem is, they are less likely to buy products made from wild plants and animals. Anyone can help. You could organize a campaign or write a letter to your MP. At a pet shop, ask where the animals came from. Say no to souvenirs such as shells and coral.

BELLA LACK (BORN 2003)

Bella is one of many young activists standing up for wildlife. As a teenager in London, UK, she began a campaign to protect orangutans and their rainforest. She put up posters, gave talks at school and shared messages on social media. Since then, Bella has done TV interviews and appeared in a film. Often she speaks about the illegal ivory trade. Bella also started a petition to ban wild animals in circuses. It worked! In 2019, the UK government passed a new law and the ban was real. Bella's message is that we must not give up hope: we can change the world, if we want to.

STOP MASSACRES

CHANGING WORLD

Not that long ago, few people had heard of climate change. Now it's in the news every day, and we realize the terrible threat it is to life on Earth. The planet is becoming warmer, which is called global warming. Extreme weather events, such as powerful storms, heavy rainfall and drought, are more common too.

HOW DO WE KNOW?

How do we know climate change is real? Studies by scientists show us what is happening. We have global weather records going back to 1880, and the last decade (2010–2019) was the warmest yet. We are seeing more T-shirt weather in the Arctic in summer. India's rainy season, the monsoon, is getting rainier. Very high temperatures are causing more megafires in Australia, California and many other places.

GROWING DANGER

Unless we slow down climate change, the danger from it is likely to grow. If crops and housing are destroyed, poor people will be hardest hit.

Rising sea levels could threaten millions of people. Flood disasters may get worse in low-lying countries and coastal cities, from Bangladesh in Asia to New Orleans in the USA, London in the UK and Venice in Italy. Some island nations in the Pacific Ocean, such as the Maldives and Tuvalu, might sink under the waves. Tuvalu could disappear by 2070!

As climate change has an impact on natural habitats, it is bad news for plants and animals. Wildlife in cold regions, such as polar bears and penguins, may suffer the most. Deserts may get larger, and rivers and wetlands may dry up. Coral is sensitive to even small changes in the sea. So warmer seas may mean that our spectacular coral reefs die off.

The good news is that activists are trying to bring climate change under control. By taking action and changing our behaviour, we all have a part to play.

Ice on mountains and in the Arctic and Antarctic is melting. Meltwater tops up the sea level, like a bath with the taps running. And there's another problem. White ice is a mirror that reflects sunshine back into space, which stops the planet overheating. When the ice goes, global warming speeds up even more.

TACKLING CLIMATE CHANGE

Why is there climate change? The main cause is how much carbon dioxide there is in the air. Amounts of this gas in the atmosphere are going up. Carbon dioxide acts like an invisible blanket, keeping Earth warm, so it's sometimes called a greenhouse gas. The more of it there is, the stronger the global warming effect.

Trees and other plants help to keep the right balance of carbon dioxide on Earth. As they grow, they take carbon dioxide out of the air. They also, like all living things, store carbon inside them. But when trees are cut down and burned, this carbon is put back into the air as carbon dioxide. So clearing forests makes global warming worse.

Carbon dioxide is released when we burn fossil fuels. These include oil, natural gas and coal. The more we burn, the more carbon dioxide is given off. For around 150 years, fossil fuels have been the main method of generating energy. We need energy to power vehicles and aircraft, heat buildings and produce electricity. As the human population grows, so does our energy use.

TAKING ACTION

All is not lost. There is much we can do to combat climate change. Above all, we can use less energy from fossil fuels and protect habitats that store masses of carbon, such as forests and peat bogs. Many activists and politicians are drawing attention to climate change. Students and schoolchildren are getting involved in different ways. One youth campaign, called School Strike for Climate (or SS4C for short), involves taking a break from lessons once a week on a Friday to raise awareness of the issues. The campaign was started by young Swedish activist Greta Thunberg (see page 45), who famously said, "Our house is on fire." Think about joining in, but do get permission from your school and parents.

XIUHTEZCATL ROSKE-MARTINEZ (BORN 2000)

This singer is one of America's best-known environmental activists. You pronounce his first name "Shoo-tez-cat". He has given many speeches in front of politicians, including at the United Nations headquarters in New York, USA. With others, he has taken the US government to court for failing to take action on climate change.

CLIMATE CHANGE SOLUTIONS

Scientists warn we don't have long to deal with climate change. After 2030, it will probably be too late to stop it accelerating out of control.

A great start is to switch from fossil fuels to renewable energy. This can come from the wind, sunshine, the movement of water in ocean tides or as it flows out of dams, and even from hot rocks underground. What's the best thing about renewable energy? It never runs out!

Iceland is the first country to get all its energy from clean, renewable sources. Many cities worldwide are now aiming to reach that target, too.

Another alternative to fossil fuels is nuclear energy. However, there is a small risk of serious accidents at nuclear power plants, and the process creates toxic waste. There are also biofuels. These are made from crops such as sugar cane and maize, and can be burned like fossil fuels. But growing them takes up land we could leave as rainforest and other wild habitats.

Wind energy is generated by wind turbines on land or at sea. A large one makes enough electricity for about 1,500 homes for a year. Solar energy is generated by metal panels, placed on roofs or on the ground in huge solar farms.

TREES FOR LIFE

Trees swallow carbon dioxide, so planting more of them can make our planet greener and healthier! Trees give off oxygen, which we breathe. They also suck up water and hold it in their leaves and trunk, which slows down how fast it reaches the ground, stopping floods. Their roots stop soil being blown away. We literally need trees for life. No wonder scientists say, "Forests are worth more alive than dead." But you don't have to plant a whole forest to make a difference. You could team up with friends and neighbours and plant some saplings in your school, street or local park.

WANGARi MAATHAi (1940-2001)

Born on a farm in Kenya, Wangari was determined to study. Despite coming from a poor farming family, she became the country's first ever female professor. Her big idea was for villages and community groups to plant trees, which would protect the soil and so help poor farmers. She created the Green Belt Movement, which has planted over 45 million trees in Kenya. For her amazing achievements, Wangari was given one of the world's top awards, the Nobel Peace Prize.

FOOD and FARMING

When you last went to a supermarket or restaurant, did you think about where all the food came from? Producing food gobbles up a lot of valuable land, fresh water and energy. Transporting it around the world burns huge amounts of fuel, too.

The diet of most of the planet's human population is based on just five staple crops: rice, wheat, maize, soya beans and sugar cane. Then there are dozens of different fruits and vegetables. Many people also eat dairy, meat and fish. But with more mouths to feed every year, millions worldwide are already going without proper meals – or even starving. The challenge of how we will feed everyone is a headache.

To produce enough food, farming today is often on a large scale. Farmers use giant machinery and spray chemicals to kill insect pests and weeds. This boosts crops massively, but harms wildlife. Numbers of insects, including vital pollinators such as bees, have crashed. Land farmed for crops is becoming worn out, since it is being used so heavily. As the soil gets thinner, it is washed or blown away.

What we eat can help save the planet. More young people are looking at the food on their plates and wondering what they can do to play their part. Here's a shopping list of things you and your family might consider.

- Choose ugly fruit, wonky carrots and knobbly potatoes (they taste just as good). Then farmers and shops won't have to throw so much away.

- If you can, avoid food flown from overseas. This cuts food miles – the distance food travels to get from the field to your fork.

- Shop for local produce. It's another great way to slash food miles.

- Support nature-friendly farming. Organic food, for example, is grown without harmful chemicals.

- Grow your own! You can grow strawberries, tomatoes, salad leaves and herbs in pots or hanging baskets.

- Reduce waste. Try only to put food on your plate you actually want to eat.

Rainforest in Southeast Asia, the home of orangutans and other special wildlife, is cut down to make way for palm oil plantations. Palm oil is cheap and it's found in around half of all household goods, from sauces and spreads to toothpaste and shower gel. But there are options free from palm oil. Check the label before buying.

FISHING

We live on a blue planet. Seas and oceans cover more than seven-tenths of the Earth. This saltwater world is home to billions of animals, from worms and crabs to whales and fish. So it's not surprising that humans have always treated the sea as a gigantic source of free food.

Fish and shellfish are a healthy choice for us to eat, full of protein. They form much of some people's diets, especially on islands and by the coast. But overfishing is a huge problem. Fishing boats and their nets are getting larger. Many are like floating factories. They sail far out to sea to catch and process more and more fish, and some fish stocks are vanishing. When one type of fish runs out, the ships just switch to catching another one.

Overfishing affects not just fish themselves, but everything in the ocean. Fishing takes away the food for many other sea creatures. The nets also trap sealife by accident. Many sharks, turtles, dolphins and seabirds drown like this. Fishing boats throw them back in the sea – what a waste.

PROTECTING SEALIFE

It's high time we treated the sea better. Governments have a big part to play. They can set up "no-take" zones, which are sometimes called Marine Conservation Zones. These are like nature reserves for the sea, where fishing is not allowed. After it stops, sealife can recover quickly. Activists are calling for many more of these zones to be created.

When you go shopping or eat out, you can help by choosing seafood that has a label saying it is sustainable. Seafood with this guarantee does not damage the environment.

SAVE OuR OCEANS

MEAT EATING

Sizzling sausages, juicy burgers, tender chicken... meat is a tasty treat for many people. What's not to like? Well, eating meat is not such a simple matter.

Some people choose not to eat any meat, and become vegetarian or vegan. This may be for religious reasons. Or it may be because they feel killing living things is cruel, or they don't like how farm animals are kept. People also give up meat due to its massive impact on the environment. Farming animals uses far more land, water and energy than farming cereal crops, vegetables or fruit. Cows use most of all. Raising cows for beef takes up two-fifths of the world's farmland. Much of that was once forest.

Beef and dairy cows are a major cause of climate change. Every cow burps and farts a gas called methane. Like carbon dioxide, this is a greenhouse gas that gives rise to global warming. One cow pumps out 70–120 kg of methane a year, and there are around 1.5 billion cattle on Earth. That adds up to a lot of gas!

24

MEATY MEALS

When it comes to meat eating, the USA, Argentina and Australia are top of the league. But the truth is, many of us eat too much meat. Every meaty mouthful puts pressure on the planet. There is no doubt that a plant-based diet is better for our world. But there are many other ways to cut down without giving up animal products altogether.

Why not plan meat-free days? Try to see meat as a luxury, not something you eat every day. There are also heaps of meat replacements. Made from mushrooms or veg, they can taste virtually the same as the real thing. Scientists are even making artificial meat in labs.

CATH RiLEY and RUTH GALLOWAY
(BORN 1974)   (BORN 1977)

Cath and Ruth from Australia are on a mission. They want more of us to try delicious meals made with insects. Yes, insects. The two mums run The Cricket Bakery. They turn crickets, which are like grasshoppers, into powder that can be used in cakes, crackers, soups and smoothies. As Cath and Ruth say, insects are a planet-friendly source of protein. Farming them doesn't take much space or energy, and they grow fast.

AIR POLLUTION

Take a nice, deep breath. It should feel refreshing! Clean air is vital for our health. But often the air is not as clean as it should be. Many kinds of human activity make air dirty. This air pollution is mainly gases and small particles, and we frequently can't see them.

Fossil fuels are a major cause of air pollution. Burning them releases carbon dioxide (see page 16), and pumps out harmful chemicals and smoke. Vehicle exhaust fumes are one example, because petrol and diesel are made from oil, which is a fossil fuel. Other examples include smoke from power plants and factories, and wood smoke from forest fires and log burners in homes.

When air pollution becomes really bad, it hangs over cities in a filthy fog, called smog. Smog makes asthma worse, and leaves us more vulnerable to colds and flu. It can eventually lead to cancer and heart and lung disease.

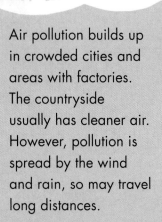

Air pollution builds up in crowded cities and areas with factories. The countryside usually has cleaner air. However, pollution is spread by the wind and rain, so may travel long distances.

CLEANING UP

Many countries now have clean-air laws, and that is largely down to protests and campaigns by activists. They demanded that their governments did something to cut pollution levels.

Cities have car-free days to take vehicles off the roads. They also ban traffic from some zones, such as in the city centre. We can help by sharing car journeys and using public transport. Another big step is to change the fuel that vehicles run on. More and more cars, buses and trucks are powered by rechargeable batteries, or by biofuel. Even better, we can get around on electric bikes and e-scooters. Could you cycle more?

Trees and other plants are on our side too, as they soak up particles of pollution. People are planting more trees and greenery to boost the air quality in their neighbourhood, especially near busy streets.

During the coronavirus lockdown in 2020, people stayed at home. When traffic disappeared overnight, so did air pollution. This shows us something. If we change how we go about our lives, fresh air and blue skies will quickly return.

POLLUTION of LAND and SEA

People are producing more waste than ever, and it has to go somewhere. When rubbish bins are collected, have you thought about what happens to it next? A lot of the waste is buried in the ground in massive pits called landfill sites. Waste is also burned and even dumped at sea.

The USA creates over 250 million tonnes of waste a year – more than any other country.

Water becomes polluted easily. Farming chemicals and fertilizer wash off fields into rivers and lakes. Chemical waste from factories ends up there, too. Sewage is another type of pollution. Most sewage is processed to make it safe. However, sometimes it gets into rivers, or is pumped into the sea. All this pollution helps masses of stinky green algae to build up in the water. The algae kills fish and other wildlife, and makes water undrinkable and dangerous to swim in.

Pollution can stay in the environment for years. If giant oil tankers spill their cargo, the thick oil kills thousands of seabirds, and washes up on beaches long afterwards. Volunteers work hard to rescue and clean the oiled birds, then release them.

Everywhere community groups are cleaning up the environment. Surfers Against Sewage, for example, was set up by surfers in Cornwall, UK, to stop sewage being poured into the sea. Many groups are trying to make us think about how we can be less wasteful.

MAKING LESS WASTE

The best solution is to create less waste in the first place. Ask yourself, "Do I really need to buy this?" If you do, are there alternatives with less packaging? Choosing organic food helps too, because organic farming is kinder to the land and produces less waste. Recycling is a fantastic way to fight waste. Paper, cardboard, fabric, glass, metal and some plastic can all be recycled. This not only shrinks the mountain of rubbish, it also reuses materials.

Share any good ideas with friends. Some zero-waste activists can fit a year's rubbish into just one jar!

METAL   PLASTIC   GLASS   PAPER

We can generate energy from leftover food, farm animals' poo and human sewage. The waste is sent to huge "digester" tanks to be turned into biogas. This gas is then used to make electricity. There are even buses and trucks that run on biogas. You could call it poo power!

PLASTIC PERIL

Plastic is incredibly useful, yet it's also a nightmare for our planet. Why? It does not rot away. Instead, it breaks down bit by bit. The tiniest pieces, called microplastics, are too small to see. Plastic lasts in the environment for hundreds of years.

Some types of plastic can be recycled, and the amount we recycle is going up as more of us take action. But most plastic is still not recycled. Much of this plastic trash ends up in the soil or sea. Plastic has even been found at the bottom of the deepest ocean. For sealife, plastic is deadly. Fish and turtles swallow it by accident. Whales and dolphins wash up dead, with stomachs full of plastic fishing nets and other rubbish.

MELATI and ISABEL WISJEN
(BORN 2001 and 2003)

These young activist sisters were fed up of seeing plastic litter all over the beaches of their home, the tropical island of Bali, Indonesia. Still at school, they began a campaign called Bye Bye Plastic Bags. Their plan was to get plastic bags banned on the island. In the end, their dream came true. Bali banned single-use plastic in 2019. Since then, the sisters have taken their message far and wide.

Ready to join the war on plastic waste? Look around your home, school or sports club, and see which things you use are made of plastic. In future, could you swap these products for plastic-free ones? Check labels, as plastic can be in things you don't expect, such as tea bags and glitter.

TO FIGHT PLASTIC WASTE, REMEMBER THE 3 RS:

Reduce how much plastic you buy and get through.

Reuse plastic objects for as long as you can.

Recycle plastic when it's finally no longer any use.

Single-use plastic is the most wasteful kind. It includes bags, bottles, straws, cups, food trays and packaging. See if you can get rid of it from your daily life. Say no to disposable straws and cups, and carry a refillable water bottle.

Eight million tonnes of plastic enter the world's seas every year. By 2050, there might be more plastic in the sea than fish.

ENERGY in the HOME

We all love nice, cosy homes, where we get heat, light and power at the flick of a switch. It seems so easy and convenient. But houses and flats use a lot of energy. Much of that energy is made from fossil fuels (see page 16). So how we live in our homes has a big impact on the planet.

Unfortunately, some of the energy used in homes is wasted. Heat can escape through the walls, windows and roof, and we turn on electrical devices more than we need to.

Modern homes are full of amazing gadgets that make our life easier. Many gadgets run on electricity – everything from ovens, fridges and washing machines to TVs, hairdryers and games consoles. Why not make a list of the gadgets you own? You might be surprised how many there are! However, in most homes, even more energy goes on heating rooms and hot water. In warm climates, air-conditioning is another major use of energy.

How energy is used in a typical US home:

Heating rooms 43%

Heating water 19%

Air-conditioning 8%

Lighting 5%

Fridges and freezers 3%

Other electrical devices 21%

Activists are calling for many more efficient homes to be built. Sometimes these are called eco homes. The best of them use hardly any energy. Their clever designs have specially insulated walls and roofs that keep in heat, and large windows that let in plenty of sunshine (so you don't need lights on as much). They often have solar panels to make electricity.

Whatever your home, there is masses you can do to save energy. Could you help your family be energy savers, not energy wasters? Try to suggest simple changes for every room. Here are some ideas to get you started:

Switch off lights in empty rooms.

Don't leave TVs and computers on standby.

Boil only as much water in a kettle as you need.

Turn the heating down a couple of degrees.

Don't open windows when radiators are on.

Run the dishwasher and washing machine on a cooler setting.

Putting up a notice or poster will remind the whole family of your mission. The good news is that your suggestions will reduce the household bills. So you will save money too.

LET'S SAVE
ENERGY

WATER for ALL

Every living thing needs water. We use water for drinking, washing, flushing toilets, cleaning things, making crops grow, in factories and to make electricity. Our bodies are over half water too!

Virtually all of the planet's water is in the salty oceans. This means only a tiny fraction of it is fresh. But it's this fresh water that people need. Although we can turn salt water into fresh water, the process burns a lot of energy and is expensive. So we must look after our fresh water supplies. They include rivers, lakes, wells and springs, where water bubbles up from rocks underground.

HOW WE USE WATER

6 litres a minute flows from a running tap

80 litres to fill a deep bath

330 litres used each day in the average UK home

7,000 litres to make a single pair of jeans

2 billion litres a day to flush all the UK's toilets

Activists are trying to make sure that everyone has enough clean, fresh water. Are you ready to join them and become a water warrior? Start by treating water as precious and using it wisely.

DON'T WASTE WATER

CLEAN WATER 4 EVERYONE

WATER IS LIFE

PROTECT OUR WATER

WILLIAM KAMKWAMBA (BORN 1987)

When William was a boy in Malawi in Africa, crops were dying due to lack of rain. He had to leave school at 14, because his family could no longer afford to send him there. Then William saw a library book about wind turbines. So he designed his own version, and built it from odds and ends that he found lying about. Next he designed wind turbines that made enough electricity to pump water for the whole village. William is now an engineer and his incredible achievement inspires other young people to solve problems and follow their dreams.

Saving water is vital. Activists are asking farmers and scientists to find new ways of farming, so less water is wasted. They say companies that waste water should get big fines. They are calling for more homes to have a water meter, so people can see exactly how much water they use.

There are many ways to be water wise. You could turn the tap off while brushing your teeth, or take quick showers, which use less water than baths. Can you think of any other simple steps to take?

EARTH ACTIVISM IN YOUR OWN BACK YARD

Gardens and back yards are awesome places for wildlife. They don't have to be big to give nature a home. Even a tiny balcony or windowsill planter in a busy city can attract beautiful insects and birds.

As people destroy natural habitats and as cities swallow up the countryside, these little patches of outside space become even more important for nature. Think about it. If you add together all the gardens and back yards, balconies and planters, they equal one enormous nature reserve. Okay, you might not be visited by tigers or other rare animals, but you can still welcome wildlife to your doorstep.

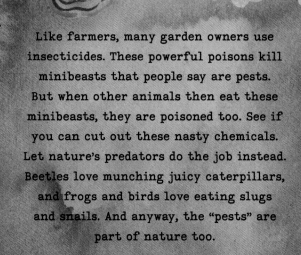

Like farmers, many garden owners use insecticides. These powerful poisons kill minibeasts that people say are pests. But when other animals then eat these minibeasts, they are poisoned too. See if you can cut out these nasty chemicals. Let nature's predators do the job instead. Beetles love munching juicy caterpillars, and frogs and birds love eating slugs and snails. And anyway, the "pests" are part of nature too.

ARE YOU READY TO REWILD SOME OUTSIDE SPACE?

First things first. Wildlife is not keen on tarmac, paving, fake grass or wooden decking. The more greenery there is, the better. Could you add pots, planters or a flowerbed or two? Choose flowers and herbs that are full of nectar and pollen for insects. Do some research first, or ask at a garden centre.

A packet of wildflower seeds can produce a mini meadow full of life. If you see a handy tree or wall, could you put up a bug house, bee hotel or bird nestbox? Neat and tidy lawns are not that great for wildlife, so leaving patches of grass to get longer allows weeds to grow. The weed flowers and seeds will attract all kinds of bugs and other insects. Finally, ponds are brilliant for wildlife. No room? Then just sink an old bucket into the ground.

If you don't have a garden or yard, are there other local areas you could help turn into refuges for nature? Perhaps you could team up with friends to create a wild zone at a school, community centre or care home.

SHOPPING

Shopping can be fun, especially choosing new things, and shopping online is easier than ever. Adverts tempt us to buy more and more. All the games, gadgets and gear have to come from somewhere, though.

Everything we buy uses valuable materials and resources. Making and transporting the goods takes energy, and it may harm the environment. Take fashion as an example. Growing cotton to make clothes swallows lots of water, and the dyes and other chemicals used in clothing factories can create pollution.

YVON CHOUINARD (BORN 1938)

Yvon is an American billionaire who owns the outdoor clothing brand Patagonia. About thirty years ago, he decided that his company must work harder to make the planet a better place. So it reduced the pollution and waste from its factories. It increased how much recycled materials it uses. Every year the company gives money to conservation projects, which it calls an Earth Tax. Today, many more companies are run like Yvon's. Shoppers choose their products because they are made in an environmentally friendly way and they treat people fairly.

Endless shopping is bad for the planet, but luckily, more people are waking up to the problems with this lifestyle. Many campaigns encourage us to be responsible shoppers. Are you one? The secret is to buy less. Only choose what you think you really need. Make those things last, then hand them on, so that other people can love them after you. It's time to persuade your family and friends: buy less stuff!

Pass old clothes and games on to brothers, sisters or cousins, or swap them with friends.

Check labels and product descriptions, so you know how things have been made.

Find out which brands are the most environmentally friendly.

Mend and repair things, rather than just throwing them away and getting new ones.

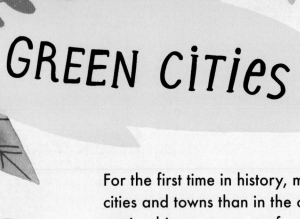

GREEN CITIES

For the first time in history, more of the world's people live in cities and towns than in the countryside. Our urban areas keep getting bigger as more of us move there in search of a job. We are building taller skyscrapers. We are creating new islands in the sea so cities can grow. By 2050, seven out of ten people will call a city home.

To make room for cities, natural habitats are destroyed. But now activists are spreading the message that cities do not have to be all concrete, tarmac, glass and steel. It is possible to make space for nature, too, so that wildlife and people live side by side.

More cities around the world plan to become green cities. But what is a green city? It has plenty of green space, including parks, street trees, gardens and living roofs (with grass, flowers and even trees on top). They have workplaces, shops, schools and leisure facilities within just 20 minutes of where people live. People can get around on foot, bike and scooter, which reduces pollution and cuts how much energy the city uses.

GREEN AND HAPPY

Green cities are happy cities. We know this because scientists have found that spending time in green space is good for us. If we can see plants and trees and hear birds singing, it relaxes us and makes us feel better. Try it and see.

Seeing nature can help us heal. Scientists discovered that patients in a hospital got better more quickly when they could see a real tree through a window. If all they could see was a blank wall, they ended up staying in hospital longer.

KABIR KAUL (BORN 2006)

Londoner Kabir loves watching the wildlife of his home city, from red foxes to peregrine falcons. He wants everyone else to enjoy London's wildlife too. So he has created an online map that shows more than 1,000 of the city's nature reserves and other green spaces. The website needed many hours of careful research and took over two years to finish. Kabir also gives talks about London wildlife and blogs about his adventures in the urban jungle. In 2020, his hard work earned him a special award from the UK Prime Minister.

Vancouver in Canada already gets nine-tenths of its power from renewable sources. It wants to do even better and be the world's greenest city.

FLYING

Humans have always dreamed of flying like the birds. In 1903, it finally happened, when the first aircraft took off. Air travel started to become really popular in the 1950s. Since then, aeroplanes have got faster and the cost of flying has come right down. People have even got used to flying on day trips.

But cheap air tickets are not entirely welcome. That's because flying does massive damage to the environment. Aircraft jet engines burn kerosene, a type of fossil fuel made from oil. As this fuel burns, it releases toxic gases into the air. It also produces masses of carbon dioxide gas. Carbon dioxide, as we have seen, helps create global warming. On top of these problems, building huge airports takes up precious farmland and wildlife habitats.

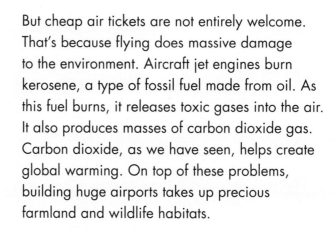

In a normal year, around 100,000 flights take off around the world each day. These create a total of one gigatonne (1,000,000,000 tonnes) of carbon dioxide gas. If we could weigh all that gas, it would amount to roughly the same as 200 million adult African elephants! It adds up to an awful lot of global warming.

If you want to protect the Earth, flying is the worst type of transport you can choose. We somehow need to kick our habit of jetting around the planet.

Some people say it is okay to fly, so long as you do something to cancel out the carbon dioxide released by your flight. For example, they say you could plant some trees that will soak up the same amount of carbon. But activists reply that an even better idea would be to plant the trees and not fly in the first place. Climate-change campaigners have other neat suggestions, too. Instead of flying for work meetings, people can easily do business on video calls, without leaving their home. Instead of flying abroad on holiday, we can take a "staycation" closer to where we live. Or take the train. Going by train is usually much better for the planet than flying. During the coronavirus pandemic in 2020, many people tried these alternatives to flying and found they preferred them.

HOPE: A GREENER FUTURE

Earth, the planet we know and love, is changing fast. It is changing for the worse, because of what we do. It needs taking much better care of, and that is down to us.

Our own decisions and actions, however small they feel, are important. One person can't do everything, but every person can do something. That includes you. As the famous conservationist Jane Goodall says, "You cannot get through a single day without having an impact on the world around you. What you do makes a difference, and you have to decide what kind of difference you want to make."

Earth Day is held every year on 22 April. It gives us a chance to think about what the planet does for us, and how we can help to protect it. The first Earth Day was in 1970, and now it has grown there are events in many countries. Make a note in your diary to join in next April!

CLIMATE
EMERGENCY

ONE
OF PLANETS
HUMANS CAN LIVE ON
100%
HOW MUCH HUMANS
DEPEND ON NATURE

SKOLSTREJK

To save the planet, we must all be activists. Write that letter, design that poster, join that campaign, pester those parents. Be the change. From being plastic clever to water wise, there is so much you can do in your everyday life. It is not too late for us to think of a better world – one where we work together with the rest of nature, not against it.

GRETA THUNBERG (BORN 2003)

It seems the whole world has heard of this quiet young climate activist from Sweden. Just mention the name "Greta" and everyone knows who you mean. One Friday in 2018, aged just 15, Greta began a lonely protest outside the Swedish parliament. She was so angry that politicians were doing barely anything to control climate change. Every Friday since then, Greta has taken time off school to carry on her climate protest. Other schoolchildren and students have joined her. Their Friday protests have become a global youth campaign, called School Strike for Climate. Greta has inspired millions of others with her bravery and her simple but powerful message. Maybe we should all be more like Greta.

FÖR KLIMATET

GLOSSARY

ALGAE simple, plant-like living thing. Usually found in water, including the sea.

ARTIFICIAL made by humans.

ATMOSPHERE layer of gases around Earth, which we often call air.

BIOFUEL fuel made from plants or animal waste. It is a renewable fuel.

BIOGAS a common type of biofuel.

CARBON a chemical substance found in all living things, as well as in coal, oil and diamonds.

CARBON DIOXIDE a gas made up of carbon and oxygen. It contributes to global warming.

CLEAN ENERGY energy that creates no pollution or waste.

CLIMATE the normal weather for an area at that time of year. Climate is measured over many years.

CLIMATE CHANGE change in the temperature or weather, compared to what you would normally expect.

CONSERVATIONIST someone who works in conservation, which is protecting other species and habitats.

CORAL tiny sea animal that often lives in a hard, rock-like skeleton. Lots of these skeletons make a coral reef.

DROUGHT serious lack of rain.

ECO HOME home designed to cause little or no waste, and use as little energy as possible.

ECOLOGICAL FOOTPRINT a measure of how much land and water we each need.

ENDANGERED when a plant or animal becomes very rare in the wild. Unless we help, it may in the end disappear forever, or go extinct.

ENGINEER person who uses science and technology to design and build things

ENVIRONMENT area where living things are found.

EXTINCT when the last member of a species dies and there are no others like it left.

FERTILIZER material used to make crops and other plants grow faster.

FOOD MILES the distance food travels from where it was produced to your plate.

FOSSIL FUEL fuel made from ancient plants or animals that died millions of years ago. Examples include oil, natural gas and coal.

GLOBAL WARMING when temperatures rise around the world.

GREEN CITY a city where renewable energy is used as much as possible, homes and other buildings are energy efficient, waste is recycled as much as possible, there are plenty of green spaces and people can safely walk, cycle and use public transport.

GREENHOUSE GAS a gas that traps heat in the atmosphere and causes global warming. One example is carbon dioxide.

HABITAT particular place where living things are found, such as a desert, forest or pond.

INSECTICIDE a chemical used to kill insects.

IVORY hard white material, found in the tusks of elephants, rhinos and some other animals.

MARINE PROTECTED AREA like a nature reserve for the sea.

NATURE RESERVE an area set up to protect natural habitats and the living things found there.

NO-TAKE ZONE an area of sea where fishing is banned.

NUCLEAR ENERGY energy made in nuclear power plants by splitting tiny particles apart.

ORGANIC farming without artificial chemicals, including pesticides and fertilizers. Natural fertilizer is allowed.

OVERFISHING catching too many fish, where fish numbers go down as a result.

PEAT BOG a wetland that grows on top of a blackish, soil-like material called peat.

PETITION when groups of people sign a website or form asking for a change to be made.

POLLINATOR an animal, often an insect or bat, that transfers pollen between flowers.

POLLUTION harmful matter that gets into water, soil or the air, which we then call polluted.

RECYCLING saving and sorting waste so it can be changed into something that can be used again.

RENEWABLE ENERGY energy from natural sources that won't ever run out, such as wind or solar power or biofuel.

SAPLING young tree, suitable for planting.

SCHOOL STRIKE FOR CLIMATE also called SS4C, or Fridays for Future – a weekly strike on Fridays, when schoolchildren and students leave classrooms to demand action on climate change.

SINGLE-USE PLASTIC disposable plastic, which is used once then thrown away.

SMOG dangerous type of air pollution in cities, like a cloud of dirty air, that is pumped out by vehicles and chimneys.

SPECIES a particular type of plant, animal or other living thing. For example, the tiger and leopard are two species of cat.

STAPLE CROP crop that supplies a big part of people's diet, such as rice, wheat or soya beans.

STAYCATION a word for a holiday spent near your home, enjoying your local area and things to do there, instead of travelling a long way.

SUSTAINABLE using things carefully so they don't run out. Sustainable hunting and fishing are two examples.

TOXIC something harmful to health, such as pollution or poison.

UNITED NATIONS an organization set up to allow meetings and discussions between the world's countries.

VEGAN a diet that includes no food or drinks made from any kind of animal product.

VEGETARIAN a diet with no meat or fish, but which may include eggs, milk, cheese and other animal products.

WEATHER not the same as climate, weather is what's happening right now, so it changes from hour to hour.

WIND TURBINE a kind of windmill, with moving blades that convert the wind to electricity.

INDEX

A
Age of Humans 4
air pollution 26–27
air travel 42–43
Amazon rainforest 9
Attenborough, Sir David 7

B
biofuels 18, 27
biogas 29

C
carbon dioxide 16, 19, 26, 42, 43
Chouinard, Yvon 39
cities, green 40–41
clean-air laws 27
climate change 14–19, 24, 45
clothes 38, 39
coronavirus 27, 43

E
Earth Day 44
eco homes 33
ecological footprint 7
energy 6, 16, 18, 29, 32–33, 40,
   41
energy efficiency 33
extinction 8, 10

F
farming 18, 20, 24, 28, 35
fishing 10, 11, 22–23
floods 15
food 20–25, 29
food miles 21
fossil fuels 16, 17, 18, 26, 32, 42

G
Galloway, Ruth 25
gardens and back yards 36–37
global warming 14, 15, 16, 24, 42
Goodall, Jane 44
Green Belt Movement 19
greenhouse gases 16, 24

H
habitat loss 5, 8–9, 15, 36, 40, 42
habitat protection 8
homes 32–33
household gadgets 32
hunting 10–11

I
insecticides 20, 36
insects as food 25
ivory trade 12, 13

K
Kamkwamba, William 35
Kaul, Kabir 41
kerosene 42

L
Lack, Bella 13
landfill sites 28
living roofs 40

M
Maathai, Wangari 19
Marine Protection Zones 23
meat eating 24–25
meat replacements 25
methane 24
mining 8

N
nuclear energy 18

O
oil spills 28
organic food 21, 29
overfishing 22

P
palm oil 21
plant-based diet 25
plastic waste 30–31
pollution 26–31, 38
population, global 6–7

R
rainforest 9, 18, 21
recycling 29, 30, 31, 39
renewable energy 18, 41
Riley, Cath 25
Roske-Martinez, Xiuhtezcatl 17

S
School Strike for Climate 17, 45
sea levels, rising 15
sewage 28, 29
shopping 38–39
Silva, Marina 9
single-use plastic 30, 31
smog 26
solar energy 18, 33

T
Thunberg, Greta 5, 17, 45
transport 27, 40, 42–43
trees 9, 16, 19, 27, 43

W
waste 22, 28, 30–31, 32
waste, reducing 21, 29, 31
water 34–35
water pollution 28–29, 30
water, saving 35
water usage 7, 34
whaling 11
Wijsen, Melati and Isabel 31
wildlife 7, 8–13, 15, 20, 28, 36–37,
   41
wildlife trade 12–13
wind energy 18, 35

DISCUSSION TIME

Imagine a typical day and think of all the things you do that have an ecological footprint. What steps could you take to reduce your footprint? Can you do any of them yourself? Do you need adults to help with others?

Are there any laws you would change or create to help protect habitats?

How would you design
a green city?

Can you think of some
different ways people
might eat less meat?
Why is this important?
What way would you
like to try?

50

How would you persuade someone to avoid single-use plastic, such as cup lids and straws? Which arguments do you think work best?

How can digital technology and the Internet help us to reduce how much we travel?

Imagine you run a factory making clothes. How might you make your factory and your clothes more environmentally friendly?

Why are trees and forests so important to life on Earth?

SCHOOL STRIKE 4 CLIMATE

SAVE TH PLANE

THERE IS NO PLANET "B"

Invent some clever new uses for empty food containers or household packaging. For example, washed tin cans could be turned into flowerpots for a windowsill.

In what ways does a growing human population put more pressure on the planet?

QUIZ

1. In 2020, how many people were living on Earth?

a) 2.6 billion b) 6.5 billion
c) 7.8 billion d) 10.1 billion

2. Which habitat is sometimes called "the lungs of the planet"?

a) the Amazon rainforest b) the Pacific Ocean c) the Great Barrier Reef d) Arctic tundra

3. What job did Marina Silva hold in Brazil?

a) headteacher b) zoologist
c) engineer d) politician

4. What activity was banned worldwide in 1986?

a) hunting whales b) having animals in circuses
c) making plastic straws
d) selling ivory

5. Climate change is making what events happen more often?

a) megafires b) flood disasters
c) powerful storms d) all of these

6. Which country was the first to get all its energy from renewable sources?

a) Brazil b) Sweden c) Kenya
d) Iceland

7. Wangari Maathai set up which environmental movement?

a) the Green Hat movement
b) the Green Belt movement
c) the Green Giant movement
d) the Green Power movement

PROTECT OUR WATER

DON'T WASTE WATER

8. Which of these is NOT one of the staple food crops that most of the world's people depend on?

a) rice b) cheese c) maize d) wheat

9. Cows burp and fart large amounts of what greenhouse gas?

a) methane b) carbon dioxide
c) nitrogen d) oxygen

10. How many litres of water does it take to make one pair of jeans?

a) 6 b) 80 c) 330 d) 7,000

11. Who designed wind turbines after reading about them in a library book?

a) Bella Lack b) William Kamkwamba c) Melati and Isabel Wijsen d) Kabir Kaul

12. When is Earth Day celebrated each year?

a) 11 March b) 22 April c) 30 June
d) 4 September

Answers: 1c, 2a (but the others are also very important in absorbing carbon dioxide and giving off oxygen), 3d, 4a (since then the others have also been banned in some places or all over the world), 5d, 6d, 7b, 8b, 9a (they also give off carbon dioxide, which is another greenhouse gas, but methane is more of a problem), 10d, 11b (the others are also amazing young planet activists), 12b

FIND OUT

Name three types of renewable energy.

Find out if your school uses green energy. If not, can you find out whose responsibility this is? Perhaps you could speak or write to them and ask them to come up with a plan.

Explore the wildlife in a patch very local to you - your garden, a nearby park, somewhere at your school, or even your street. See what animals and plants you can spot, and find out what they all are.

How many kinds of organic food can you find in your local supermarket or grocery store? Is the labelling easy to spot and understand?

Name an endangered species of animal or plant for each of the world's seven continents. What are the main threats putting it at risk of extinction?

What types of electric or battery-powered vehicle have you seen so far? What advantages do they have over other vehicles? Are there any disadvantages?

Go on a plastics hunt around your home, or in a single room. How many plastic products can you spot? Would you swap any for plastic-free alternatives in future?

Which activist in this book would you most like to find out more about? Do some research of your own and write about them in the space here. You can draw a picture if you like!

GET ACTIVE

What three things would you do to try and look after the planet and make sure other people did too?

How would you do it?

What are your hopes and dreams for a healthier planet?

Activist actions

VOLUNTEER! Pick an organization that works for equality or helps marginalized groups, and find out what you can do to support them.

WRITE A LETTER! If you see an example of inequality happening, find out who has the power to make it better (a politician, the head of a company, your school headteacher) and write to them. Write your request clearly and respectfully.

START A PETITION! This is like writing a letter, but you tell lots of people about it and persuade them to sign it, too. You can gather signatures on a physical letter on paper, or set up an online petition.

HOLD A FUNDRAISER! Why not hold a bake sale, sponsored bike ride or concert to raise money for a cause you care about.

BUY FAIRLY. Try to become aware of how the things you buy are made. Do the companies who make them do their best to take care of the environment, or are they harming animals and habitats or polluting the air, land or sea? You can choose to buy things produced in a way that respects the planet, or boycott things that harm it. Boycotting something means refusing to buy it as a protest.

SAVE WATER! Try to come up with some neat ways that you and your family could save more water, and draw up a list to discuss with them. Many actions are easy and cost nothing, while others might require you to buy a simple device, such as a water saver to put in your toilet's water tank.

TRAVEL SMARTER! Get together with some of your school friends to see if there are any ways you could make travelling to and from school better for the environment. Draw up a list of your ideas to show your parents or schoolteachers.

Take inspiration

Look back at the examples of child activists in this book and what they are doing to fight for the planet. Can you think of something similar that you could do?

TAKE PART IN A CITIZEN-SCIENCE SURVEY. These are simple surveys you can do in your garden, park or local area, which involve doing things such as looking for and counting certain animals or plants. Usually you can report your sightings online. Many wildlife and conservation organizations run these surveys, so check their websites.

CREATE A WILD SPACE. Ask your school or your local library, hospital or care home if there is a small corner that you can help make a bit better for wildlife. You could offer to put up nestboxes for birds and bees, or add some colourful flower planters to attract insects. This is something to do with your family and friends.

GIVE A SHORT TALK on one of the subjects in this book. It could be for your class at school, or for your Brownies or Cub-Scout group, for example. You only need talk for a few minutes.

GET CLEANING. Find out about organized beach clean-ups in your area, and take part to help save ocean wildlife and seashore habitats.

PLANT A TREE. Planting a native tree makes a big difference, making homes for wildlife as well as helping in the fight against climate change. Look for a scheme near you for help with choosing and planting.

USE TECHNOLOGY. It can help you find out what actions to take. For example, Giki is a free app that lets you scan your shopping (food, toiletries, cleaning products) and find out if they are made with the environment in mind – or suggest a better alternative.

WRITING and DRAWING ACTIVITIES

Design a green home. What special features would your green home have? What would it look like?

Use this space to design a poster, T-shirt or tote bag for an environmental cause important to you.

Create a menu for a meat-free meal
that your whole family can enjoy.

Write a short speech about one of the subjects in this book, which you would give if you were elected as a politician.

Design a new logo and paint scheme for an electric or battery-powered bus, or a truck that runs on biofuels.

Design a fact file about a rare animal that is under threat and needs our help. Include information such as its size, where it lives, what it eats and any of its interesting behaviour. You could also add a drawing of the animal, or find a photograph online and then print it out to trace over or stick in.